MORE THAN BLOOD KIN

Twice adopted

Siblings Separated by Adoption
but United by God

J. MIKE HIGGINS
(siblings contributed to their chapters)

Dedication

This book is dedicated to all
who have faced similar or
different challenges and to all
who have been abused, neglected,
misunderstood, abandoned,
or adopted.

Table of Contents

Acknowledgment

All of these four individuals and their families that have emerged from them are to be thanked and commended for being a part of each sibling's life— past, present, and future.

I would also like to thank my grandaughter, Morgan Kent for typing the original manuscript.

Introduction

The following are *true* stories, over fifty years in the making, about four siblings: two sisters and two brothers who were each adopted by four separate and unique families of different social, economic, and religious backgrounds.

The names used are the original names given to them at birth though each sibling's name was changed at the time of adoption and for privacy reasons have not been revealed.

The purpose of sharing these stories is not for the sake of sympathy, nor are the subjects to be considered victims.

The true purpose is to learn from these four life stories the effect of not having an intact family and the results of being adopted, both good and not so good.

Acknowledgments

All the participants of these four individuals and their families that emerged from them are to be thanked and commended for being a part of each sibling's lives past present and future

Chapter 1

Oldest sibling, Brenda," Which Way Did They Go?"

I was told by my adoptive mother that I was adopted when I was around two weeks old. My birth mother had become pregnant without being married, and her father sent her to Nashville to an unwed mothers' home. Her mother asked if she might adopt me because she had fallen in love with me. My grandfather didn't want to adopt me but went along with the plan anyway.

So, my grandmother and grandfather became my mother and father. I would see my birth mother and brother occasionally but not regularly.

I was told that I had sister!

All I really knew of her was that she had blonde

hair, and her name was Sarah.

I also remember a single photo of her as an infant. I don't remember seeing her in person during my life as a young adult at any time.

I also knew I had two younger brothers that I did get to see because they lived in the same area I lived. They lived with our birth parents. Sometimes I was able to play with them.

My adopted dad worked on the L&N Railroad. So we traveled

frequently and lived several places like Colombia, Tennessee and New Orleans, where we lived quite a while. While living there as a child, I seemed to get myself in trouble—especially with other children. When this happened, my dad would always correct me with the board of education. On the other hand, my mother would always console me and pet me. As I think back on this, she probably went overboard with the petting and consoling me, so much so that it caused problems with her husband, and they ended up divorced. So my mom and I moved back to Knoxville, Tennessee to live in a one-bedroom apartment that was close to where my brothers were living. Again, I would get to see them, and also I would get to see my birth parents. My birth dad was not well and did not work. He would take care of my brothers while our own biological mother worked. (Note: My biological mother and youngest brother's adopted mother-to-be all worked at the Knoxville Glove Company.

My biological dad encouraged our biological mother to let a couple of women who worked at the glove factory adopt my brothers. The results as I know them are as follows: My oldest brother was to live with one of the ladies, but that didn't last long. My younger brother was adopted by the other lady and her husband who lived in the Knoxville, Tennessee area.

Later, when I was with my mother, we were in Miller's Department Store, and I saw my younger brother again. At that time I was not aware of where he actually lived. When I saw him, I tried to tell him he was my brother but was not permitted to by his adoptive mother. I do not remember seeing him again as a child.

After I began school, I don't remember having any close friends. I do remember feeling like everyone was making fun of me because I was overweight as a child. Of course, I would remember chants like "Fatty, fatty, two by four, can't get through the kitchen door." Others' lack of accep-tance and criticism really hurt my feelings to the point that I

15

didn't feel that I belonged any place in the world. The only person that I ever felt really cared for me was my adoptive mom.

When other children did want to play with me, I just wanted to retaliate and hit them. I was angry because they had stuff I didn't have. They had a family— which was something I had always wanted. We didn't have a car or go on vacations; we didn't have things like others had. I only had the love of my adoptive mom but, of course, I did have that. At that time, my mom developed physical problems and decided to put me in a home for kids. It was devastating to believe I had to leave the only person who had shown me any love. However, she promised to come get me as soon as she got better. While staying at the John Tarleton Home, I suffered from tonsillitis and afterward the measles, and my mother's sister came to help me and stay so my mother could go back to work. So I continued to live with my mother and her sister for quite some time. Then another family member would come around and when he did, I would be punished. I would be accused of becoming like my mother and was threatened with placement in a juvenile detention home. This escalated to the point that I began to believe it, and I had no self-esteem. I was so discouraged; others at school made fun of me and called me names. Now I felt I didn't even fit in or accepted in any family. Somehow,

17

I made it through all this negative drama.

My aunt began to play an important role in my life, but she died not long after that. Before she died, however, I became good friends with her daughter. Because I didn't get to participate in swimming or other sports like other kids, I started not liking school, but my cousin helped me get through these times. We finally moved into another home after my uncle helped us get a house; even so I never felt like I received any positive influence from him.

By the time summer rolled around, I met a guy and became pregnant. At least he agreed to marry me, so we started life together pregnant and living upstairs in an apartment above my mom and dad, who were actually my grandmother and grandfather. Note: my grandfather had actually come to live with us again.

Things didn't go so well, and he left. During the separation, he paid child support, which I later used to pay the hospital and doctor bills. After our daughter was born, we decided to make our marriage work, and we moved out to be on our own.

As strange as it seems, I didn't really know him that well. I was confused about what I should do, but things weren't so great with Mom and Dad, either. So we decided to try to work things out.

We were able to begin to put things behind us, and things got better. Not long after that, I

19

became pregnant again. This time we had a son. Unfortunately, he contracted pneumonia and died. As every mother knows, that was devastating. We did make it through this grief and went on to have two more sons. My husband began to have drinking problems after the death of our second child and also the death of his brother. Once again, there was more stress and heartache in our home. So I just made the best of what was not such a good situation.

I always wanted an intact family, to just be together, just to be a family. The alcohol problems continued, but I tried to make things work, I should say, with things as they were and not as I'd hoped they'd be. After years of this hard life, through the influence of a cousin, I attended a church. There I found what I'd been looking for: peace within myself.

It was at this time that my mother became ill and subsequently died. Again, this was a devastating time. Losing her at this point, I began thinking about my youngest brother who lived with his family in the East Tennessee area. I was able to get his mother's phone number, and one Sunday afternoon, hoping he would be there, I called their home.

His mother answered the phone and explained he was not there but lived with his family not far away. I asked her to tell him that if he wanted to talk to me to call me back. Later that afternoon, he did call, and we were able to talk for the first time as adults. We talked about things as they were at that time. He said he was a pastor of a church, and I told him I was attending a particular church. Our conversation was cut short because both of us needed to leave to get to our church services on time. Later, on a Wednesday night, he showed up at the church I was attending. I would have gone to his church, but I was afraid that my husband wouldn't understand. All of these years I had had no contact with my siblings, so to avoid conflict, I stayed away. This was the first face-to-face meeting between me and my younger brother since I was about eight or nine years old when I saw him briefly at Miller's Department Store.

During our visit, we inspected each other's eyes, noses, feet, hands, and dimples, and talked about a little of the past. He knew very little about most of our past, such as having another sister. I found that he wasn't told about anyone else but having another brother.

After this initial meeting, we were able to talk on the phone several times. However, this did not last long. My brother felt that contacting me was causing problems with his wife and also causing tension between me and my husband. Therefore, my brother, not wanting to cause anyone prob-lems, decided it was best not to talk often. We would seldom see or talk to each other.

After a couple of years, we talked about the possibility of trying to find our other siblings. I discovered that a letter needed to be sent to the state department of vital records in Nashville to request that they contact our siblings to tell them that a sibling was looking for them. Then we had to wait because they had to decide for themselves if they wanted contact with us. The first to respond was our sister who was living in New Jersey. She had three sons and a daughter. I was able to talk with them on the phone. This was an exciting time for me. My brother was able to travel to New Jersey and meet our sister and her family. I wanted to go but was afraid because, again, my husband was unsure of all these new people coming into my life.

My sister was able to travel a little later, and I was able to meet her daughter and youngest son who came with her. After her visit, I called my biological mother and told her I had met with my sister. She seemed pleased. So the next time I talked with my sister, I told her I would like her to get together with our biological mother. However, my sister was hesitant about doing this since she had not been around any of the family like I had, having been adopted from birth. She did, however, reluctantly say she would meet with her. Not long afterward, our biological

25

mother came to town with her husband (not our own father). We decided to go to the morning service at my brother's church. Keep in mind that my brother did not know any of this was taking place. So you can imagine the surprise when he looked out to see several strange people sitting in the pews. Afterward, we all went to lunch together at our sister's aunt's house. The visit was cordial, but my sister and brother were very cautious about the whole situation and not very accepting of our birth mother. Neither my brother nor sister had had any contact with our birth mother since infancy. They didn't know her like I did as I had a distant relationship with her but a continuous one, nonetheless.

The next sibling to join the fray was our other brother. I had had very little contact with our oldest brother. My first contact with him was when I picked him up at the Knoxville airport. He came home with me, and later my younger brother picked him up from there. My older brother did not have a lot to say while visiting. I felt that maybe he was ashamed of where I lived. Since I had initially talked with him on the phone, I knew he had been raised in a well-to-do family and was educated. I was able to overcome the rejection I felt at this time, realizing that I might not have had all the things he grew up with, but I was loved

27

by my adoptive mother and that's more important to me.

You can have all the money in the world, but, in my opinion, if you don't have God, you don't have anything. I thank the Lord that I have found my sister and brothers. I thank God today that he helped my husband stop drinking and helped our marriage last over fifty years.

Chapter 2

Sarah " Somewhere Out There"

To be adopted can be a good thing. It affects everyone differently. You are always wondering who you are and whether you did something to cause this. You're always looking for answers. Some people can cope with this better than others.

This is my story of what happened to me. I was given up when I was an infant. I was placed in an orphanage where later my adoptive parents came and picked me out of a lot of babies. They told me that I was very special when I was around two or three. I'm not sure I really understood that I was adopted; I was very young, and they tried to assure me that I was very special. They had wanted children and had tried for so long but couldn't have any naturally. That's when they decided to adopt.

Mom said when they came to the home and saw me, she knew I was the one.

I was a chubby little blond-headed baby with dimples. She said they just fell in love with me. My dad had just gotten out of the Air Force, and my mom was a stay-at-home mom. They worked hard before they got me, and Dad

made pretty good money. We lived
in a nice, big home in a prominent area of town. We belonged
to the country club, and they
had me in all kinds of activities. I liked playing piano, tap
dancing, ballet, and swimming
all the time. Anything I wanted
was given to me. I was just plain
spoiled. I was a daddy's girl
even though I think that caused
a lot of tension between them.
When I was about four or five and
going to school, I began asking
questions about being adopted.
Mom would just say she loved
me and then change the subject.
That confused me because I wanted
to know.

When I was six, my mom and dad
came to me and said they had good
news. Mom was going to have a

baby. Well, good news for them was a nightmare for me. My heart dropped, and I got very sick. I had been the only child for all this time. I was scared and hurt and believed they wouldn't love me anymore, thinking I would not be their special girl anymore. While they were getting ready for the new baby, I was doing anything I could to get attention.

The baby was a boy. After he was born, I thought, "Well, this is good. I can still be a daddy's girl." So much attention was going to him that I had to do something. I would try to flip the crib or make the baby cry—anything to get rid of this problem. But all that did was get me into more trouble—it didn't work. Then I figured that if I helped them, maybe I would fit in. So I started helping with him, and we formed a bond. I just didn't feel loved or wanted, and I wasn't that special girl anymore. Then I started school and had a lot of friends. They would ask how it felt to be adopted. They thought it was cool. I would just say it was all right and hide my true feelings. I was not sure just where I fit in!

Well they got us a nanny, and I became very close to her. She understood me and helped me through a lot of my pain. We did a lot together. Then one day, Mom said that we were going to move. That really upset me. To leave was very hard and confusing, but I couldn't do anything about it. "Can the nanny come with us?"

I asked. They said yes. Then I found out we were moving up north. Well, here I was, being adopted and being a southern girl going north. I was not sure how that would work. After we moved to Illinois, I found out we had to send our nanny back. She could not stay. They wouldn't tell me the reason. All I knew is that it upset me so badly.

Starting a new school was hard, but I was looking for new friends. I began settling in, but I had to answer all the questions about being adopted. Why was this so hard for people? I felt like I had the Plague.

Mom became sick and had to have back surgery. She wanted to have it done in Tennessee where her sister could keep my brother.

That meant that I had to stay with dad. I had been helping with my brother, and it just seems like he would get in trouble and nothing would happen. He'd just get a slap on the wrist. Not me though—I guess because he was a baby and I was older.

I had a good friend who lived across the street. She really cared about me. I spent a lot of time at her house. I had more and more questions, such as who am I, where did I come from, who was my biological mother, and did I have siblings? She would help me to find out. I was always looking for something.

One day, when I was helping my dad cook dinner, he asked me to sleep in his room. I thought that was strange. Then I thought maybe it was because Mom was away and he was lonely. At that time I was maturing and getting my once-a-month friend. Mom never told me about that so when it happened, I was scared to death. I had to call my dad into the bathroom because I didn't know what to do. Dad gave me a Kotex and said, "You're all right; put this on. You will get this once a month."

I didn't understand, but I did what he said. About a couple of weeks later while I was sleeping, Dad got into my bed. He went to give me a goodnight kiss and started touching me. I pulled away and said, "No, this isn't right." I was so scared and started to get up, and he said just go back to sleep. Why did he do this? I knew I'm not his real daughter, but he raised me. I went into my own world and tried to just stay away from him. When Mom returned home, I told her what had happened, and she got mad at me and said to forget it. What did I do? I didn't understand. I felt so alone and unwanted.

Then, a week later, I was told I was going to a private school for kids who have problems. So, off I went but didn't stay there long because I ran away. While I was away, my parents moved to New Jersey. So when I came home for a short while, it was to a new home. There they put me in counseling. I met a few people while I was at home.

Then I was sent to a hospital where you are locked up. You have to earn your way to another area where you can have more freedom.

I met the best doctor who really helped me and saw what was going on in my life. He put me into the area where I could attend school. My parents wouldn't even come to visit. They were ashamed of me. It was very hard for me to under-stand why they adopted me. My self-worth was gone. I tried to kill myself by taking pills and drinking bleach. I was taken to a hospital in Oslo and recovered. After a year there, I returned home. For a while, things were better. I had gotten a job and met new people. My parents, got me to meet this boy, who was the son of some of their friends.

We were just friends and hung out together; I had met this

guy at my work whom I knew from school a while back. I really liked him, but my parents told me to stay away from him. He really liked me, too. So I would see him at work. One night, my friend came to pick me up to take me to his house. He is the boy that my parents liked. My parents were at his house, visiting his parents. On our way there, we got stopped by a roadblock. The guys pulled my friend of the car and started beating him up. Then they grabbed me and took me into this dorm. I was kicking and screaming as they threw me on this cot. All I saw was men everywhere. One got on top of me while another was tying my hands down. I couldn't breathe. I was so scared. I knew they were going to rape me, but I must have passed out. All I can remember is running out the door into the arms of the police. They took me to be checked out at the police station. My parents were called, and my mom was there. My dad was out of town. The police wanted me to identify them and press charges. My mom said no and to let her take me home.

I couldn't believe she would not let me do that. She was embarrassed. I didn't do anything wrong. She made me feel so low and bad about myself. How could she love me? Again, was this because I wasn't her true child? What was I to think? We weren't close, anyway. I tried so hard to be the daughter she wanted.

I began seeing the guy they didn't like. After a few months of dating I found out I was pregnant. I was so afraid to tell my family. All I knew I was going to have this baby no matter what. After they found out, my dad went to my boyfriend and asked him what his intentions were. Of course, he was scared and young and did not know what to do. Well, Dad gave him an offer he couldn't refuse: never see me or the child again or get married. The next month, we got married. All my brother would say is she's adopted and not really a part of his family. That really hurt me. Being married wasn't all that great, but it got me out of the house and gave me my precious daughter. My husband and I began

41

to grow closer, and the love was there. The next year I was pregnant again and had my first son, and I had two more after losing two. My life was always in turmoil, but I had to prove I could keep it together. I tried to be the best wife and mother I could be.

At that time my parents and brother moved to Vermont. Dad had bought a ski resort. We would take the children to visit on vacation. Mom and I finally began to have a close relationship.

It took me getting married and having children to get close to her. I was happy about that. I tried to spend as much time with her as I could. She really began to trust me and would tell me her problems. That made me feel good that she could confide in me. Our last visit there was awful. My brother tried to make a move on me by kissing and touching me. It upset me because he was my brother. He said, Well you're not my blood." At that point my husband grabbed him and told him to stop. Then I found out my mom was real sick and had cancer. She didn't have long to live. I tried to spend as much time with her as I could.

The same year my daughter got pregnant. She was only sixteen and didn't know what to do. I didn't want her to put the child up for adoption, and so I offered to care for him. Then my mom passed away. It was hard to get over the loss, but I had a new baby boy to take care of. I felt that maybe this was my purpose of being alive. My marriage was failing, and there wasn't anything I could do but to take care of my three boys and my grandson. My daughter had moved out and married a year later. At that time my first husband and I separated. We remained friends for the children.

Then one day I received a letter from Nashville. They were looking for a woman who was born on my birthday, lived in Tennessee, and had my maiden name. They were looking for me! I was so overwhelmed! I was shaking and crying. Words couldn't describe how I felt. It took me a while to calm down. Then I had to ask myself what I needed to do. I had called my dad to tell him, and he told me to tear it up and forget about it. I couldn't do that! So I called the phone number on the letter.

A woman answered, and I told her who I was. She seemed surprised, so I told her that I got this letter and was calling the number I was given. Then suddenly she called to someone in the background, "It's Sarah!" For the first time I heard my given name. A man got on the phone and said, "I'm your brother. I have been looking for you for a long time." After talking for a few minutes, he told me I had a sister who was the one who told him about me. She had tried to find me but because of the fact she was not adopted out, they would not give her the information. So she went to him and told him about me and another brother who they were still looking for.

All of this was a shock to him because he didn't know about us. We talked for a while; then he gave me my sister's number. I called her, and I was so over-whelmed an excited. I have a sister! I have always longed for one. After we talked, I just wanted to meet with them in person. I couldn't wait to let everyone know of this after all these years. I was thirty-nine and finally had a family. Now I felt like I belonged. We kept in touch, and then my brother said he was coming up to see me. I was so excited but also scared. My life was in turmoil, and I was afraid he wouldn't like me.

I was ashamed of myself but did want to meet him.

Well he came and brought his daughter. I was so happy and felt so at peace for the first time in my life. What a good, loving man he was and handsome, too. We had so much in common and even our physical appearance was similar. This was amazing. His daughter was so pretty and looked so much like my daughter.

During all of this, I was still in touch with my sister who I really wanted to meet. I decided to fly down to Knoxville, Tennessee, and meet her and her family who now was my new family. I knew I could stay with my aunt who has always been supportive and helpful whenever I needed to talk. What a strange feeling I had inside. Is this really happening? Well I did fly down, and my sister met us at the airport. I had taken my daughter and youngest son with me.

My sister had her husband and sons with her. They took me to my aunt's and we talked, hugged, and talked more. Then they had to leave, but I would see them the next morning. We were all going to church together. My brother was a preacher.

I could not believe all of this. I had trouble sleeping. The next morning, we all met at the church. As my brother was giving the sermon, I felt a hand on mine. I began shaking and was so overwhelmed. Tears were streaming down my face. It was my biological mother. I was so afraid to look, but I did. There she sat, just staring at me. I became angry and confused, yet this is the woman who had given birth to me. This has really changed my life. I now had a mom, sister, two brothers, and there were nieces and nephews to meet.

We have a lot of catching up to do. We also need to get to know each other. I already know that I love them all, and I am so thankful that we can now be a family—that is, of course, if that's what they want. I know that's what I want because I have been searching for them all my life.

So now it's time to start a new chapter in my life with my new family. I wonder how this new journey is going to turn out. A lot more is to come.

When I returned home all I could think about was my new-found family. I was having trouble with my marriage, and it ended in divorce. After months of trying to get things together, I decided to sell my house and move to Knoxville. Leaving the past behind was so hard for me. I still had children at home, so they had to come with me. My oldest boy was turning eighteen and wanted to stay. So he got his own place with my help.

I had started a new relation-ship with a good man, and he was willing to help me move. After we got to Knoxville, he decided to stay, and we have grown closer. He helped me with the boys. At

that time I had three with me,
ages 17, 12, and 4. The youngest
was my grandson that I have
raised from birth.

My father also came along to
help us get settled. When we got
there, my sister and family came
over to help. That made me feel
so good. It took a lot of time
for us to establish a relationship. We were so different yet so
much alike; after time we found
that out. Through the years, we
really got to know one another
well. I became very close to my
brother and also to my sister.
Our lives were very different.
That was the hard part; I still
wasn't sure if I fit in. It's
very hard when you're looking
for something that may not be
there. I still hadn't met my

other brother, but they had. That hurt me a lot, but it's okay. We would get together on holidays or birthdays for the kids. My children met their children, and it was strange how we had more in common than we knew.

Finally, after several years in Tennessee, I was going to get married again. We have been together for such a long time that I finally gave in and said yes. This was awesome because my first marriage was not very big and very rushed by my parents.

I got to have my brother marry us, and my sister was the maid of honor. My daughter, sons, nieces, and grandson were all in my wedding. My adoptive brother gave me away. My aunt took my mom's place, and it was beautiful. I felt so loved and really happy for the first time in my life. This was my real family, and even though some were missing, they were in my thoughts.

A few months later after we were married, two of our grand-daughters ended up living with us. One was two and a half and the other was fourteen months old when, at that time, we didn't know we would become permanent parents.

I have now gotten to know my family and love them more than they realize. We talk and get together a lot, but of course we have such different lives. I wonder if things would have been diffcrcnt if we had been together from the start. I'm sure it would have been. I wonder if not knowing about my adoption would have changed things. Of course, it would. I just have to be thankful for what I have—I am blessed and love them all. I will continue to get to know more about them; that is, if they let me.

Thank you for letting me share my story with you. This has been a remarkable journey. I went through so much pain and hurt but also so much love and happiness.

Chapter 3

It's a Wonderful Life

Here is a brief biography of Steven Michael Johnson:

Born: January 23, 1950, as Stephen Michael Johnson, Knoxville Tennessee

Birth father: Theodore Johnson, Sharps Chapel Tennessee

Birth mother: Mary Elizabeth Linde of Kentucky

One brother: Tony

Two sisters: Brenda, Sarah

Adopted: 1954, to Harold and Kathleen Jones, Jackson Tennessee

Adopted sister: Suzanne Jones, also adopted.
Married: 1976, divorced 2003
Children:
Stephen Jones, deceased (drug overdose) 08/26/2005
Hunter Jones, married, three children
Catherine Long, married, three children

As I approach my 65th birthday, I am sharing and reflecting my life experiences as an adopted child.

My earliest memory begins during a hot summer sometime about 1952 or 1953. I recall a red brick structure with a dirt yard. People were sitting all around the yard. I was playing on a sidewalk with other chil-dren. There was an ice cream truck coming down the road. We are all given cups of the ice cream to eat. I remember that when you would pull off the top of the cup, there were pictures of baseball players printed on the lid's underside.

My next memory was being transported one night up a hill to a building. I entered the building with a person, who placed me in a chair in the lobby. I looked back for the person who came with me, and the door loudly slammed shut. I was then escorted up a long staircase into a room full of loud kids. There were lots of kids in bunk-type beds. The kids were dressed all in white t shirts and white underwear. It appeared this is where they all slept. That is all I can remember up to June, 1954.

I remember playing in the yard on a sunny day. The house was next to a big ditch with a wooden bridge stretching to the other side where there was a barn that housed a huge black horse that screamed all the time with a loud neagh. I had just gotten back from my walk up the road to see the neighbor who gave me cookies she called biscuits that I equated to biscuits for dogs. I think this was a farm, and I was living with a foster family. I do not remember any people. I heard that someone was coming that day, so I knew that I had better hide if someone came. By surprise, they arrived. When I heard a car drive up, I immediately jumped behind a yellow-and-white check-ered chair. Within minutes, I was caught, scooped up, and put in a car, traveling somewhere. I crouched down in the backseat floor board of the car until I became curious to peak out the window. As I looked up and out of the window, I noticed that we were going over a green bridge. I could see water below, and the green pickets on the bridge raced one after the other in front of it. Then it was all over, and the car stopped in front of a big brick building. Later in my life I would travel the green bridge going to and from classes when I was a student at the University of Tennessee.

The driver opened the door and told me that we were going into the building. There was a beautiful wide open space in the building, and the man sat me down on a couch. Within seconds, a nice woman arrived and said hello. The driver turned to go and left me with the woman. I was then taken to a room in the building. In that room were two older people and a young girl. I was then introduced to my new family. I was told that I was going to spend some time with these people, and if it all worked out, I could stay with them for a while.

The young girl's name was Suzanne. She was almost six years old. Within minutes, we bonded and immediately began to throw a beach ball around, laughing and playing. I was asked if I would like to go see the Indians at the Indian reservation, and I was in agreement. We hopped in the car and left on my first road trip. We had a great time in Cherokee, North Carolina.

A couple of days passed, and the man and woman asked if I would like to come live with them and Suzanne in Tiny Town, Tennessee. I was taken to a small town in western Tennessee. I didn't have any idea this was 400 miles away from where I started. I agreed to go, and off we went. I never looked back.

My new life began that day upon arriving in Tiny Town. I longed for nothing. I was immediately introduced to new friends, a healthy diet, my own room, a loving family, and my new best friend—Suzanne. I was placed in a safe home with every advantage. After a year in Tiny Town, the Jones officially adopted me and gave me my new name: Harold Steven Jones. My father is Harold I. Jones, a prominent grocery man, and my mother is Kathleen Jones, who is a homemaker.

I started school in the fall of 1956. I liked school, and I advanced on schedule. I loved all sports. Suzanne was a tomboy, so we played everything together. As I grew up and I went into the 4th, 5th, and 6th grades, I began playing flag football and little league baseball. I seemed to excel in sports and lost interest in school very early in my life. As I moved into the 7th grade, peer pressure began to influence my behavior. My grades suffered to the point that I became academically behind and I had to repeat the 7th grade. At this time, I had begun to drink alcohol and smoke cigarettes in order to get noticed by the popular kids.

My bad grades caused me to lose out on several school privileges like playing sports. I was thirteen years old and thought I was twenty-one years old. I wouldn't listen to anyone and relished being the bad boy. My parents tried to help me, but I thought I was not out of control. I was going to have it my way at any cost—then I began to get in trouble with the police. At this point, my parents could not handle me, and I was sent off to an elite private boarding school outside of Nashville. At this point I had gotten very far behind in my core subjects. I had failed most all of the subjects that I was taking.

I was now almost two years behind in school because of English. That summer, I was not allowed to come back to Jackson, so my parents sent me directly to Nashville to Castle Heights Military School to attend summer school. I was fifteen and a half years old, partially still in the 7th and 8th grades. Upon arriving at Castle Heights, I met a new friend. His name was Rocky Rue. He was a swell fellow who was my age, and we immediately became friends. After a fist fight or two, Rocky straightened me out and encouraged me to "just get through it."

Shortly thereafter, my dad sent me a medallion in the mail. On the medallion was a little prayer, and he asked me to read it every night before bed and every morning when I got up. It read: "God, grant me the serenity to accept the things that I cannot change, the courage to change the things that I can, and the wisdom to know the difference." I did as he wished, and things began to change. That summer, I was able to take enough cram courses (that the school provided for troubled kids) to get caught up in school and made straight As. I was then able to return to Jackson. I was a new person with ambition and goals. I attracted new friends (probably because I was driving to the senior high school that went to the 9th grade back then. There were no middle schools in Tiny Town).

While I was gone, Suzanne had become an all-western Tennessee basketball player. In today's world we would call her a high school all-American, but after high school there were not any college sports available for females. Suzanne graduated in 1966, went off to college, graduated, and began teaching middle school P. E. in Florida. She still lives in Florida with Pat, her partner.

I got through junior high school and started high school in 1967. I had finally begun to be a normal seventeen-year-old kid. I began playing sports again, making the high school football, basketball, and baseball teams and receiving honors in each. I began to participate in several school clubs, and I was elected to be president of my high school student body. I participated in church activities and acquired leadership roles in teen activities. I graduated from Tiny Town High School in 1969.

In the fall of 1969, I enrolled in the University of Southern Mississippi. I tried out and made the USM basketball team. I pledged a fraternity and participated in several clubs and activities.

I had always wanted to attend the University of Tennessee in Knoxville, Tennessee. So I gave up basketball at USM, and in the fall of 1970, I transferred to UT.

During this time, I dated a girl from Jackson. We thought that we were really in love. She was still in high school in 1970 and '71, and we would go back and forth seeing each other. And in 1972, after high school graduation, she decided to come to UT. After a few months in the spring of 1973 (because I was to graduate soon), I asked her to marry me, and she said no.

It devastated me, and I began to drink and party heavily. As the result of my self-pity, during the next six months I hardly took a sober breath, not knowing that I was already a functioning alcoholic. I met another girl, Susan, who will reappear later in my story. I graduated in August, 1973. Upon graduating, I returned home to Jackson, Tennessee and went to work for a local bank. I advanced through the pecking order of the bank for a couple of years. My drinking never subsided.

In the summer of 1975, I was running with the rich adult kids who were a socially active and privileged crowd in Tiny Town, spending most leisure hours at the lake drinking or at after-midnight parties on weekends. On a few occasions we partied in the middle of the week. I can remember going to work drunk and two hours late. I was the assistant branch manager, and that didn't go over well. One girl in our group attracted me sexually, and we began to date. With my alcoholic mind set and the lack of responsibility, I fooled myself into getting engaged, and we married in the summer of 1976. Shortly after the wedding, I think we both knew that we had made a mistake.

Divorce in the '70s was an unacceptable thought. Although we thought that we loved each other, we were never in love; the idea seemed to be a good idea. We drove each other crazy from day one because we were two very immature and spoiled brats. We co-existed, and then in 1978, our first child, Stephen, was born. Then in 1980, our second son was born. My wife had a miscarriage in 1982, and then our daughter was born in 1984. Up to that point, we had done pretty good job of faking a bad marriage, and although the marriage offered very little, we adored our children. Throughout those first eight years of marriage, I flittered from job to job, never finding any career satisfaction or making very much money. This pattern lasted for the next twenty-five years, as we were constantly borrowing money from my parents.

As the children grew up, we discovered that our love for them had replaced any personal fulfillment in the marriage. We had become resigned to the fact that it just was what it was and tolerated each other as long as we could. As the children's teenage years approached, our parenting disagreements were reflected in the behavior of the children. We could never agree on any way of raising our children.

Each child graduated from high school and went to college; Stephen went west to the University of Montana, Hunter to Ole Mississippi, and Catherine attended the University of Alabama and Ole Mississippi. Stephen and Hunter graduated while Catherine was still at home. During Catherine's senior year, we separated and then divorced. The divorce proceedings lasted two years. They were two tough years.

During the years we were married, we had lived a very high life style and constantly had financial problems. After our divorce, the alcohol overwhelmed

me for the next five years. I
was stopped by the police for
drinking three times in 2005 and
let go; then I got three DUIs
between 2006 and 2007. I lost my
license for five years, committed
a felony, and I was in and out
of jail nine times for drinking,
spending eighteen months in
jail until 2010. In 2005, my son
Stephen was found dead in Denver,
Colorado, from a drug overdose.
In 2007, I was in jail the night
before my daughter's wedding and
missed the most important date
in her life. I was so ashamed.
She was and is still crushed.

During the years, I have developed a wonderful relationship
with my natural brother, Tony. He
has waited patiently for our time
together. He is the best brother

anyone could ever want. We met in 1986.We try to see each other as much as we can. I have only met with my birth sisters on a few occasions. Hopefully, we will find more time to get together. I see Suzanne about once per year. My adopted father died in 1999, and my adopted mother passed in 2004. I threw away and lost most of my inheritance in the divorce. My birth mother is still alive and lives in Macon, Georgia. We write letters and talk on the phone occasionally. We have not seen each other since 1954. My birth father died in 1952.

Since 2010, I have turned my life over to Christ. I have not had a drink since August 1, 2008. I have rekindled a relationship with Susan, who I mentioned earlier, and we are engaged and building a new life and a new home in Georgia. She is wonderful. She knows about everything in my past and accepts it unconditionally. She is my rock and my soul mate. I have been able to work odd jobs to supplement my Social Security and pay my bills. I have six wonderful grandchildren. Things are much better, and I am sober! God is so good!

Over the years, many people have asked me about how I feel about being adopted. I feel that my adopted parents provided a wonderful life for me. I was told immediately, at four and a half years of age, that I was adopted. They were always very up front about how I was so special. My adopted mother constantly reminded me throughout my life that adopted children were chosen by their parents. She made me feel so valuable, safe, and loved. My adopted parents taught me to endure through faith, not to worry about anything, and to honestly believe that everything would be alright. I view my adoption as a blessing.

Chapter 4

Only Child or Baby of the Family?

This chapter begins with the youngest of the four siblings who recalls his life growing up in east Tennessee.

I began my life as Anthony Wayne Johnson. I do not remember any of the details of my earliest years because I was only eighteen months old when I was adopted. Therefore, I have to rely upon the accuracy of the facts later told me by both my adoptive mother and a dear aunt who would be to me an anchor and wonderful supporter whom I could turn to up until her death in 2010. The couple who adopted me were much older parents as compared to the age of the parents of other children my age. I would wonder why, as a child, that my parents did'nt adopt me sooner, thinking that they wouldn't be so old and would be younger like all the other kids' parents. At that time, the question of why wasn't I born sooner had not occurred to me. I was told that my adopted mother worked where my birth mother did. So when my birth mother decided she could no longer care for me, she decided to place me for adoption. My to-be-adopted mother could not

have children of her own due to
health issues. So things were in
place for her to adopt me.

Looking back to not only my
situation but to what I learned
later about my siblings, I have
come to realize that God was
actually orchestrating each of
our futures. As Joseph in the
Bible told his brother after they
had mistreated him and sold him
into slavery, "You meant it for
evil, but God worked it for good."
Also in the New Testament, Paul
wrote, "All things work together
for the good, to them that love
the lord and are called to his
purpose." Back to what I was
told as explained by my mother.
Around age six or seven, I was
told that I was adopted. Up until
that time, I was unaware of any

of the adoptive processes or any other birth parents or siblings. All I remember asking was two questions that I continued to ask for years to come and would not be reconciled for more than twenty-five years later.

The first question was why? I was told that my birth father had died, and my birth mother was not financially able to provide for me. My response and my feelings, however, were personal. I began to feel worthless, not special, not valuable, and not needed. These feelings would become an intricate area of the fabric of my life.

The second question was aimed toward my adopted parents after discovering I had a brother. The question was again: why? Why didn't they adopt him, too? I was told that he had been taken to another home. At that time, I had a difficult time accepting this information and felt so alone and empty and hurt that the adoptive parents or somebody could not have kept us together. I do not remember longing for or looking for my birth parents before or since. From that day forward, I constantly wondered and looked for another boy who looked like me, with the same nose, jaw line, dimples, flat feet, and so forth. Sometimes I would think I had found him but was disappointed over and over again. However, I never gave up looking for him. It would be many years later when I would find that not only did I have a brother;

in fact, I also had two sisters.
It has been difficult to believe
that all the lonely years as an
only child growing up by myself,
that I could have had not only a
brother but two sisters to have
shared my life with.

Telling my story is not an
attempt to invoke pity or sympathy, and it is not to play
the poor-me syndrome or victim.
However, it is an attempt to
share true heartfelt disappointments and hurt and grief in order
to relate to you and others who
have experienced similar events.
You are not alone. My road or
path traveled was not free from
emotional, physical, and major
internal self-esteem issues that
would be unpacked throughout
my younger years and continue

on into the later years of my adult life.

I would like to say for clarification purposes that I will refer to my adoptive parents as Mom and Dad. I cannot say I remember anyone who cared for my needs as they did. Both have been deceased for over thirty years. I must say I was loved. I appreciated their time, care, and the provisions provided. Both my parents worked, and my grandmother on my mom's side was at home each day, when I arrived home from school. My grandmother, or "Mama," taught me about God and Christian faith more than anyone else. If you were fortunate to have someone like that, acknowledge them and thank them for loving you enough to share their time and faith.

Needless to say, we spent much time together, and Mama spent a lot of this time praying for me. The house we lived in was small with a tin roof and only two bedrooms. Therefore, I slept in mama's bedroom. She had a full-size bed, and I had a small half bed in the corner of the room until I was around fifteen years old. It would be then that I got my own bedroom. It was in an attempt to accommodate me; my parents actually moved out of their own bedroom into the den onto a couch that folded out into a bed so I could have my own room. Even though I was excited to have my own room at the time, I didn't realize the sacrifice my parents were making for me. However, within about four years,

they would be back in their bedroom, and I would be married and
living somewhere else.

In general, I believed that my
life was normal. I made average
grades in elementary school,
started playing football around
six years of age, and liked to
fish. In the summer, I would go
on vacations and get to visit
my aunt and uncle on their farm
where I would enjoy playing in
the fields and barns and fishing in
the two adjoining creeks. My aunt
would play the guitar and sing
old gospel hymns. Even though I
was the only child there, I had
a great time and never wanted to
leave. Sometimes we would visit
my other aunt and her children
in Georgia. I remember them as
good, hospitable people but I

never felt like we were kin. I always felt like a visitor or guest and only liked going to visit because we usually rode the train to get there.

The following events are real feelings. The shame, hurt and worthlessness I have dealt with for more than forty years is real. Imagined or realized, maybe they were both, but to me they were and are real to me. If I had not had the good loving Christian family who loved, supported, and guided me along the way, the things I'm recording in this chapter could have been more difficult at the time and could have had a much greater impact on my life. I'm thankful through it all that God has protected me and helped me to deal with ongoing issues even today.

As I came into my adolescent years I began to have a problem of wetting the bed. I understand there are others who also had this problem. Of course, my parents were concerned and in an effort to help, sought medical and professional advice. At first, they were advised to watch my intake of fluids which meant I would not be allowed to have anything to drink after 8:00 p.m. Another opinion was to not allow me to stay up past 8:30 p.m., another was no water after eight and more sleep as prescribed. However, this did not affect the frequency or amount of times I continued to wet the bed. I was frustrated and embarrassed and sensed that this did not please my parents, especially my dad.

The medical sources felt that I was too lazy or could have a problem with sleeping so deeply that I could not wake up to get up and go to the bathroom. My dad would get me up march me into the bathroom and swat me on my bottom and command me to pee. This began to be a habitual exercise night after night; it seemed like an eternity. I began to resent this event in my life partly because of the shame, partly because of the pain, and partly because it didn't achieve the objective. I still continued to wet the bed. A glutton for punishment I wasn't. I did not do this for attention or any other reason. I just could not seem to wake up before the deed was done. I was so frustrated and discouraged; even when I was able to go to a friend's house I would do it there too. Even after futile attempts to not go to sleep, I would initially nod off and wake up wet. I did not want to be embarrassed so I would not ask to go to a friend's house anymore. In an effort to finally help me, my parents found and purchased a device to place in my bed. This device had an alarm that was like an alarm that is used to warn an entire community of an invasion or attack. Talk about an abrupt awakening!

Here is some insight on how this monster worked, the part that actually was placed in the bed was like two window screens, the screens were to be covered with pillowcases. A person would lie down on them. They were not particularly uncomfortable. Then, when any moisture saturated either pillowcase, it would cause the underlying metal screens to have contact with each other through the moisture. When the contact was made it sent a signal to the alarm. The alarm would sound and wake up the person. The idea behind this is after a few times, this would program the human brain to not want to go through this again.

I would like to say that all of this worked; however, it did not. Night after night I was not hearing an awfully loud alarm, but an announcement that says, I've done something terrible and not normal. To me it was not an alarm but words I heard: he did it again. I could not take the embarrassment and shame another night. I was able to find a way to stop the noise. Since I could not stop wetting the bed no matter what, I would stay awake until I was sure that everyone in the house was asleep. I would then turn off the machine. I had gathered a supply of extra pillow cases and had them hidden under my bed so I could slip the wet one off and the dry one on .Then I would turn the machine back on. As far as everyone else was concerned, there was no alarm and no wet bed. All is well. I don't know if a movie that was on television actually helped, but the movie was about a boy who wet the bed and whose mother exposed his problems to the world, which was devastating to him. I actually cried when I watched this movie. Soon afterwards, about at about fourteen years of age, I stopped wetting the bed for good. Thank God.

Along this same line of accepting responsibility and blame, another episode happened in my life at a community pool. I'd love to go to this community recreational building. As I was swimming, I had an accident. I pooped in my swimming trunks. Before I could get out of the pool, it floated to the surface, and of course I was embarrassed. As I tried to retrieve my property, the lifeguards saw it and ordered everyone out of the pool. Then all the children were lined up, and one by one, we were asked if we had done this. When I was asked, I was embarrassed and afraid. I first said no, but when the management threatened to close down the pool if someone didn't confess, I admitted it was me. I was banned from the pool. Of course, I was ashamed, humiliated, and devastated. I knew what I did was not good, but everyone was made aware that I had done a terrible thing. I decided never again would I be blamed for anything. I would do anything to avoid being blamed or being responsible.

This caused me to believe I had to do everything perfectly. Soon I realized that I could not, so I would not even try to do many things because if I did try, I would fail. Therefore, I would spend many years not excelling at what I could have. Because I would be responsible, it would be my fault; I would be considered irresponsible, not capable, shameful, and not worthy.

In short I started depending upon others; they could take the responsibility of doing things without any reflection on me. So I relied on the others around me to take responsibility.

This was almost natural since my mother was a very giving person. She did everything for me. I enjoyed the convenience of not having to do many things. All I had to do was mention something and wait; most of the time they would be done for me.

This, of course, did not help me realize my personal responsibility growing up. A word to parents here. I believe my mother loved me and intended the best for me. Unfortunately her care and generosity and my feelings about things only enabled me to stay the scared, scarred, and spoiled little boy I was.

I was never placed into the position of being responsible. This made it harder for me later in life as I did not know how to fend for myself. After I had been married for nine years, my mother developed a brain tumor and died at age sixty-six. I finally had to do things on my own. Although I had my wife, I no longer had my mother's support that I had relied on for so long.

A note to parents reading this: hear me out. Love your children but do not enable them. Help them cautiously, share your wisdom, and give them advice. Don't cover up or gloss over their mistakes, and encourage them to be the best they can be.

As I began high school and was over wetting the bed, I continued to have self-esteem issues. I became more aware that I was not liked or accepted by others. I felt that for anyone to be my friend, I would have to do something or give something to them. Therefore, when I was given things, including money, for Christmas or birthdays or any occasion, I felt that I needed to give it to others to have friends. I did not think it was possible to have friends without giving or doing something. For instance, I once received a genuine leather football I had really wanted, but I gave it to a boy at school. When my parents asked what happened to it, I told them it had been stolen at school. This upset them very much. This soon became a pattern for me and continued to be an issue for most of my life. This has caused me to not value things like most people do. To a certain degree, this is a good thing as it has kept me from being materialistic. In other words, I can give things away without reservation.

During high school, life for me was carefree, I had little interest in school and more interest in sports and girls. Or, was it girls and sports? Anyway, my attitude toward studying lacked desire and motivation. I spent my time playing ice hockey and dating girls. To me, school was only the means to an end, speaking of end, like end of school. Anyway, I maintained good enough grades to graduate.

Then a most important thing happened! I saw this beautiful young lady standing in front of the trophy case at school. Wow, I thought, if I could get her to like me as much as I liked her. I would end up being the most fortunate guy around. She did respond positively, and we began dating our sophomore year. This girl, my sweetheart, the one whom I love with all my heart, did accept the challenge.

We married after graduation. By 2014, we have been married for forty-five years.

We have two adult children and several grandchildren and great grandchildren. I would like to say that our marriage is perfect. However, I now know that no one has a perfect marriage. We have had a tolerable marriage most of these years. I was inundated with issues that I will discuss later, and she tolerated me. Early on, I did my share of drinking alcohol and acting out. After a couple of years, we almost did not make it. Two factors changed the outcome: one being a praying mother who asked God to stop me, and t he other being God stopping me and setting me on a different course.

Again, my gracious wife, tolerated my stupidity and sinfulness and forgave me. Again, I wish that I could say that things changed completely, but I can only say that life continued as has our marriage. It was not without problems but to a degree has improved.

Another example of feeling like I had to buy relationships was in high school. I worked in a local restaurant and made fair money. Of course, I felt that I would use this money to purchase friends and girlfriends. As you can imagine, a pattern of giving to others to be accepted was ongoing. It would be much later that I began to realize that most others would ride the gravy train that I provided until they got what they wanted or it ran out, and then they would move on. I know that may have bordered on being insane, but I will have to say that I have spent years doing that, knowing that I was being taken advantage of. I didn't care because I felt that I had to do it to be accepted and to have friends.

I'd be a doormat just so you'd love and appreciate me. After all, why would you ever want to be my friend? My value, worth, and self-esteem to me was almost a non-factor.

On the other hand, I have come to the realization that my adoptive parents, no matter their reason for adopting me, were loving and caring people. They had a choice, and they chose me! I came with no guarantees or warranties. They took a tremendous chance on what might have turned out to be a wrong decision. For me, it was the best thing that could have happened. I had shelter, food, love, and stability.

I am thankful for all those who are willing to take a chance on another human being instead of letting them be institutionalized or aborted.

Chapter 5

Recap and Review

When I first met Brenda, she was married with several children whose ages were close to my own children's. Her husband was a hard worker at the local bakery, and she worked cleaning houses.

Imagine if you can, both of our families having no one significant in our families, except our children or adoptive parents. Neither of us had siblings to grow up with. So when we met and began an effort to have a family relationship, it was difficult at first. Here we are blood kin, sister and brother, and had never had any lasting bonds or relationships. Brenda's husband and family and my wife, by the way, whose name is also Brenda, and our children had to get used to having other people come into their lives, also. If we were to have an intact family, we would have to adjust or not. The first couple of months were the most trying times. After several attempts to make it work, I decided to back off. We stayed in touch via phone but rarely got together. It was when years later when we thought we would try to get in contact with our two other siblings.

After contacting the department of vital records in Nashville, Tennessee, we learned that we could send a letter, and they would forward the letter to them if they could reach them. After we did this, all we could do was wait. It was two months later when we heard back from our sister Sarah. A month later we heard back from our brother Steve.

After being contacted by Sarah, I was able to arrange a trip to go to New Jersey and meet her. My daughter came with me to visit her and her children. Our visit consisted of comparing appearances and general conversation to try and get to know each other better. With Sarah, there was less tension than during Brenda's and my first meeting. However, once again, we had to get used to more additions to the families: cousins, aunts, and uncles. So it was still an adjustment for all.

Sarah worked as a tele marketer and was separated from her husband. It seemed it was the best time for us to come into her life. Shortly after our meeting, Sarah decided to move to Tennessee to begin a new life, having an opportunity to become a family—something none of us had truly experienced. Brenda was the only one to have a memory of my brother and me early on before we were taken out of the home and adopted. The next or last sibling to be reunited with the rest of us was Steve. By the time I met Steve, plans for Sarah to move to Tennessee were almost finalized.

Steve was very tentative about contacting anyone after he received the letter from the state. He wasn't sure if the letter was a prank or a real request. Steve's wife encouraged him to call. He finally called, and after we talked, he made arrangements to visit my house. He came alone, and a similar meeting took place as had taken place with Sarah. We compared our appearances, which were very similar. It was uncanny. It was like I was looking at a mirror image of myself. I also took him to visit with our eldest sister Brenda. It wasn't until much later that he would meet Sarah.

Steve was a stockbroker and had been in many business ventures throughout his life. He was married and had three children. Due to his social status, he was cautious about getting involved with me or with our sisters. After all, he had never thought about people showing up claiming to be his siblings. Therefore, he did not take the time at first to spend much time with any of us.

After meeting me, he realized that we had to be brothers. It was obvious by observation and even the way we stood and the way we talked. However, what reassured him must have been what he saw or felt when he stayed the night at my house. My parents had died, and I inherited my grandmother's house that they had lived in. It was a small country house, and we had just moved there not long before his visit. I was in the process of renovating the house to add an extra bedroom to the two-bedroom house. The walls inside of the house could be seen, and the insulation was exposed, but the room itself was the best I had to offer. So this is where he slept.

At the time I was a pastor of a small church, and contrary to popular belief, I wasn't making money. However, my wife worked as an RN at a local hospital, and we made it fine.

All of the above might have influenced Steve's opinion of me; I'm not sure. He expressed to me that I should get out of the situation I was in and that I could do better. Of course, it was my decision to make, and later he gave me a choice. He had been researching a meat-and-seafood franchise and said he would furnish the funds if I would manage it and do the hands-on work.

The opportunity was to finally be with my brother. At least that's the way I saw it. So I decided to leave the church and go into business with him. At first, it was like leaving the world as I knew it. But after the reality had set in, I realized I had made a sad mistake. The dilemma was that I didn't want to disappoint my brother, but I knew I was disappointing my God. After dealing with it for about four months, I finally called my brother and said I was sorry. Of course, he was not happy, but we closed the business two months later. I knew up front that my calling was with

God and that the business would not succeed. I only wanted to have a viable relationship with my brother and would have done anything to achieve this.

After a period of time, Steve reached out to help me financially. He offered me a manager job in a restaurant in Pickwick, Tennessee. Since I left the ministry, I had no job or income. So I turned to him again. I moved to take the job. After two months, it didn't work. Again, my calling was to serve God. So I have made some mistakes for which God,

Steve, and my family have forgiven me.

So years later, after meeting all my siblings and their families, and after remembering birthdays, spending time together, laughing, and talking, we are just doing what normal families would do. We are still learning from each other. We stay in contact and try to have an annual Christmas dinner together. We are still a work in process.

Something worth mentioning happened during the time we were all trying to adjust to each other. We also tried to form a relationship with our birth mother, who had stayed in contact with our eldest sister. It was decided we should all try to meet with her. I was left unaware of these plans. Those who made the plans though, since I was a pastor, they, being the two sisters, birth mother, and aunt, would surprise me at church and then go to lunch afterward.

Prior to this, I had never met my birth mother. So, I was very surprised that Sunday morning when I came to preach, seeing my sisters sitting with several strangers in the pew of the church. I would not know until after the service was over exactly who the others were.

As far as I was concerned, these people were mostly people with whom I had had no contact. So, for the very first time, I was being introduced to other blood kin. I did not know how to react or what to say other than to be cordial. What happened next was awkward.

After meeting at church, it was agreed that we would meet at a local restaurant. Several people showed up at the restaurant. There were three or four tables placed together to accommodate to everyone.

After finishing our meals, conversation took place involving everyone around the tables. The atmosphere was tense to a certain degree. Much was said that I had no clue of. It was different to see all the people who had similar physical features as my own. I don't know why to this day that I had never had a previous desire to find out about these people especially our birth mother. I do not mean any disrespect towards anyone, but what happened at the end of this dinner event left me speechless. The birth mother announced that she and her husband needed to get back home. She pushed away from the table and started towards me saying, "I need to give my son a hug before I go."

Immediately I felt that is not what I wanted. I felt neither disdain nor love towards her. Her actions towards me were not mutual. I lacked that mother-son bond that we should have had. Even to this day, we have little communication, and I do not regard her as my mother.

Chapter 6

The *What if?* Game

As a minister for over forty years, I have found that most people go through the *What If* scenario. In fact, as a younger man in my twenties, I found myself in what I call the *What if?* game.

During a period of about three years, when my mother died only months after being diagnosed with a brain tumor, I questioned:

What if the tumor had been found earlier?

What if they had used a different medication?

What if she had a different doctor?

Only three years later, I found my dad lying dead on his bedroom floor.

What if I had checked up on him sooner?

What if I had found him in time to take him to the emergency room?

Most of us have or will go through similar scenarios.

What if I lived in a different town?

What if I had brown eyes or darker skin?

What if I was taller or stronger?

Would it had been different?

The answer to this last question is we simply don't know. Why? Because it happened the way it happened, and we'll never know if those things, being different, would have changed anything because they weren't different. So we must live with what happened and come to understand it as it is. Since none of the What if's was what happened, we must reconcile ourselves that we don't know if it would have turned out any different. Therefore, we find ourselves in these situations because the what if's never happened.

The four siblings are actually blood kin. We are all connected by the same DNA. The oldest sibling had the expectation of having an intact family and the possibility of having other siblings to interact with.

The next child was born out of state and had never been introduced to the original family. She was adopted almost immediately to a family who would later birth another child of their own. She had no knowledge or contact with any of us until she was an adult.

The third child was born when the eldest was three. He spent time with the original family and foster care. Not much of a relationship was established with the family at that time.

The fourth child was born six years apart from the eldest. He stayed with the original family until eighteen months of age when he was adopted as an only child to an older couple.

In an old classic, B-Gee's song, "In a Room Full of Strangers," some of the lyrics in particular seem to bring all of the siblings and respective families together after many years of no contact and being reunited about 20 years ago.

Each sibling and family brings many years of traditions, needs, likes, dislikes, and hurts, both internal and external, into this room.

Chapter 7

Expectations

Children have expectations to have a good and loving mother and father.

Husbands and wives have expectations of each other and their children.

Employers and employees have expectations that when not met could bring great sorrow and separation, but when expectations are met, there is great joy.

Someone has said, "If you don't expect anything, you won't get disappointment."

Lisa Kleypas who wrote Love in the Afternoon said, "You are your own worse enemy, if you can learn to stop expecting impossible perfection, in yourself and others. You may find the happiness that has always eluded you." The following is an overview of the expectations that each of us had at the time of initial contact with the others. The fact that we are blood kin doesn't necessarily mean that everything will fit like a piece in a puzzle. Like a puzzle, each piece should fit, but if one or more is missing, putting together a puzzle is difficult.

Some puzzles are easy to work, and some are difficult. Some puzzles can be worked in a short time; others take a while.

In the lives of these four blood kin siblings, even though we share very similar likes and dislikes, our physical DNA alone does not constitute a viable sibling relationship.

The broader picture is that of our own individual families. Like a puzzle, there are many pieces, that is: sons, daughters, aunts, uncles, cousins, in laws, and outlaws.

Needless to say, it has taken some time to put four siblings with families together.

In fact it's a work in progress, even to this day, considering traditions, faith, likes, dislikes and expectations!

It has been said, "Expectations are the root of all heartaches, especially expecting too much." We build expectations of what others should be like and how others should behave. It has been said, "Stress, frustration, disappointment, anger, and irritation come from expectations" and "The secret to happiness is low expectation." In addition, "expectation is a belief that someone will or should achieve something or that something will happen or be the case in the future."

The first sibling, Brenda recalls that she spent years throughout her younger life just thinking about the past: a time when her brothers were around and when she missed seeing or spending time with her sister. She was always wondering where they were and how they were emotionally and phys- ically. Were they happy?

What did they look like now as they were adults? Would she even recognize them?

Did they survive their child- hood; were they still alive? As one can see, Brenda, the one who experienced having a family even for a short time and was the one who had a more vivid understanding of the past still had many expectations as well as questions to be answered. Her greatest expectations were to simply find the answer to the aforementioned questions with the hope or expectation to one day be a family again!

The next sibling, Sarah, recalls

As I was sitting by my window, I began thinking about my expectations of meeting my new-found family, not knowing to really expect. All I knew was that I was longing to belong to a family that would really accept me and love me for who I am! I was also wanting to find out why I was given away.

I was so excited to know that my sibling was looking for me. This made me feel wanted. When I came to meet my youngest brother, he shared with me that I also had another sister and brother. I expected that we might be able to grow close and be a family. So many years had gone by. I was not sure about how this would all work out, and I was a little scared about what might happen. What if they didn't like me? I would be crushed!

When we did finally meet, it was very hard. I had a love for them already. Their lives were so very different than mine. I tried very hard to become involved with them and their families. Sometimes I didn't feel like I would fit in.

This bothered me, because I guess I thought we would just fit, like we had been always been together. I felt that I really had to try very hard to get close to them. It was amazing how we look so much alike. We seemed to think alike for the most part, too.

I adore my sister and love her so much. I only wish that

we had had a chance to grow up together. We are still working on our relationship.

My youngest brother and I seemed to click from the start and have a great relationship. I love him, and I know that he loves me. My adoptive brother, who I grew up with, really didn't care much for me, even though I loved him. Therefore, meeting my real brother helped me through the disappointment of my adoptive brother who I grew up with. I met my older brother but have not seen him much since we first met. I'm not sure that he really wants to get to know me.

I have love for him and think he's cool, but I'm not sure that we will ever bond the way that I would like for us to. Since all of us have met, we have had an opportunity to find out things that we did not know about. We are still working together to bond and share our lives. Of course all this takes time.

To be adopted is not as great as people may think. At least for me it wasn't.

I am grateful for the parents I had. They gave me a chance to be a part of a family and took care of me, even when things weren't so good. I don't know if my life would have been different if I hadn't known that I was adopted. I know that I feel that I would not have blamed myself or gone through the heartache that I went through.

I know that now I feel more loved and that I belong to this

family. We are still working on our relationships. At least everyone seems willing to continue having a sibling relationship. It doesn't always work that way. Just be careful when you open up your heart that you don't get hurt.

Life is very funny. As Forest Gump said, "Life is like a box of chocolates, you never know what you gonna get."

The next sibling, Steve, recalls never having any desire to pursue his roots.

I was very happy with who I was, and I was very satisfied that I could be happy "living the life" without ever knowing anything of my past. My ex-wife's encouragement was the only reason I answered the inquiry from the state of Tennessee.

I guess you would say my expectations were very low.

After meeting my brother and one of my sisters, curiosity began to set in, and I began to enjoy all of the information that I held secret in my soul. The information about my birth parents began to fill in the holes of curiosity. The information about each parent whetted my appetite to know more about why I had a big nose and curly hair. One of the physical things that I immediately noticed was that my brother and I had identical hands. I gravitated to my brother not because I disliked the only sister that I had met—I didn't ! I think it was because

I had grown up with a sister and never had a brother.

After meeting my brother's family and spending very little time with them, a great fear came over me in that I was not being honest in my desire to continue the relationship with my new-found brother or sisters. (I felt that I was opening a can of worms, and I was terribly scared.) I was wrong! Several years went by, and there was very little contact.

After I divorced and my life was in the tank, I chose to turn to my brother for help. He opened his heart and came to my rescue. He has been there for me ever since. I was totally broke, and he gave me a place to live, food to eat, and transportation to job inter-views. He sat up with me endless hours and shared his Christian faith. My brother taught me that I was worthy and gave me hope that my sins had been forgiven through Jesus Christ. He helped me recognize that we are all born into this world as sinners and that no sin is greater than another.

He instilled within me the desire to learn more about the Bible. He encouraged me to look into the Book of Romans, chapters 7 and 8 that made me recognize that there is no perfect human life. My brother and my faith in Christ allowed me to change my old life and look to heaven for all of my needs and desires. In all, it was all worth finding my roots!

The last sibling, Tony, recalls his expectations as follows:

As the youngest sibling, many of my pieces of the puzzle were missing. I did not know about any siblings other than my brother. I had little to no knowledge of my birth parents. I did not know anything about our health history. As I grew older and would have a physical, I was asked about family health issues such as diabetes, heart issues, high blood pressure, or cancer. So after all siblings had met, we asked each other about all the aches and pains, as well as any known health history. It was discovered that we all seemed to have foot problems. In fact, two had foot surgery for the same reasons. All siblings have eye problems and wear glasses.

Of course all of the information was of great help to me and also to my children.

My expectations were to find out health history and find out more than I knew.

I was an only child in my adoptive family, but I was the baby of my original family. So I've had a difficult time through the years of my life trying to discover who I am. Finding my siblings actually gave me a place to start. I wish I had found out the things about myself earlier in life. Suffice it to say that I began to see and understand things about myself as I observed my other siblings. I just saw myself in many ways that I did know about me, and I did not like what I saw in myself. I would call it self-examination! I have begun to work on myself as I have come to better myself. At the age of sixty-four, I'm a work in progress!

We have had some disappointments along the way, but we have learned to step back and slow down as we have learned about each other's likes and dislikes. We are trying to be involved in each other's lives.

Having no real gage and no real expectations of what to expect, I will say that we have, for the most part, done as well as we could have. We are and will continue to be a work in progress. Our puzzle is much more complete than any of us would ever have imagined twenty-plus years ago.

Chapter 8

"Afterword'

More *than* *Blood* *Kin* is a paradox in life. In the Christian faith we are blood kin. Through Jesus Christ, we are brothers and sisters in Christ—a part of the family of God. We have faith in the blood of Christ, shed for each of us, that places us in the family of God.

In life, in general, being blood kin doesn't necessarily mean that we have a relation-ship or that we even know one another as brothers or sisters. Therefore, we submit ourselves to the fact that being a brother or sister or family member is more than blood kin. Any lasting relationship must be more than legal, more than contractual, more than just making a living or getting by, and more than being wealthy.

The fact is that being blood kin as much as one might think is important, could be of little importance whatsoever. In this book four individuals, all blood kin, have told their true, unembellished, life experiences about being taken in by outsiders, non-blood kin families who supplied sustenance, care, values, education, shelter, and a certain degree of love. Through each adoptive family's sacrifices, care, and concern, each of us who were adopted, were given a chance to have a family. So not being in a blood-kin family, we were given a certain degree of love and acceptance.

Although all of us were blood kin, we were never raised together or shared any of those experiences of being siblings. The point is that being blood kin is not so special if there is no relationship, caring, or love involved. Not being blood kin and being adopted is special if there is a true relationship with care and love.

The purpose of telling the bare truth of our stories is basically two-fold. First it has been a tough experience to recall our experiences and put these thoughts into words. To share how we have felt and thought has begun the process of healing and restoration. We have learned how much alike we are in so many ways. We also have learned more about these lives we would have never known. The second purpose of writing this book is sharing our own thoughts and feelings to connect with you. Our hopes is that you'll be encouraged and receive guidance from sharing our experiences.

Adopted or not, you may have been ignored, neglected, abused, not accepted, or misunderstood.

We understand and care about how you feel; we have been there and done that. All four of us have found a friend in Jesus Christ; we are blood kin. We are double-blood kin. We have the blood of our parents and brothers and sisters, and through the precious blood of Christ, we have been adopted into the family of God.

Life could have been, should have been, and would have been different by being an intact family. There could have been memories and should have been great times together as well as times of trouble and discipline. Instead of looking back to what might have been, we are now looking to what is and what will be a time of new relationships together. We are brothers and sisters. We are family.

Chapter 9

Adoption Defined

I would like to take a moment to take this time to share a more vivid account of adoption which is described in the Holy Bible.

A general truth taught in the scripture is that adoption is placing a believer as an adult son into God's family and giving him access to all the privileges that go with it. Therefore, a believer becomes a member of God's family by regeneration. A

Christian is literally born in to God's family by regeneration.

In the scripture, adoption is a position. It speaks not how a believer became a member of their family but of the fact he is already a member because of regeneration. God places him or her in the position of an adult son with rights and privileges[1]. At this point we might ask how adoption became available and necessary in the first place. Well, scripture explains this in Romans 8:15—16 and Galatians 4:4—6.

God's justice requires payment for each of our sins. Jesus Christ's death on the cross was the payment to deal with our sins. His shed blood and death fully redeemed each believer and made regeneration and adoption

More than blood kin

available and possible to all
who will accept the sacrifice and
believe in Jesus Christ.

The scripture describes in
detail the privileges of adoption.

The believer has a Father who
loves him,[2] cares for him,[3] pro-
tects him,[4] corrects him[5], and
promises never to leave him[6].

The believer is a fellow cit-
izen with other saints and the
household of God[7]. He is also
an heir of God and a joint heir
with Christ[8].

The believer now has within
the "Spirit of adoption (Holy
Spirit)" [9] who bears witness in
his or her heart that he is God's
child. The spirit will also raise
us up at the second coming[10].

God has predestined the
believer to be conformed into

the image of Jesus Christ and has promised to openly reveal us as his son or daughter[11].

The main emphasis of adoption is the day when Christ returns and redeems the saint's body, making it like his glorious body[12]. In that day, God shall openly show all creation to those who are his adopted children[13].

Spiritual adoption is realized as being different inside, accepting sonship, and bearing witness to others through the power of the Holy Spirit[14]. Adoption is realized through being different as we choose to live for Christ[15], becoming a child of God[16], and correction and discipline which requires us to live different from the world[17], similar to the

relationship between an earthly
father and son[18].

Verses referenced:

1 John 3:2

1 John 4:4

1 Peter 5:7

Romans 8:31

Hebrews 12:5—11

Hebrews 13:5—6

Ephesians 2:19

Romans 8:17

Romans 8:17

Romans 8:11—17; 1 Corinthians 15:5—52; Galatians 4:4—6; Philippians 3:21; 1 Thessalonians 4: 13—18

Romans 8:29; Ephesians 1:5

Philippians 3:21

Romans 8:23; 1 Corinthians 15:38—58; 2 Corinthians 5:1—4

Galatians 4:5—6; 3:26—37; Romans 8:14—17

1 John 3:1—2

John 1:12—13

2 Corinthians 6:17—18

Hebrews 12:5—13

If this book has related to you in
any way, please communicate with us.
Send any correspondence to:

P.O. Box 996,
Kingston, TN 37763